MW00948389

# My Dog THOR

# My Dog THOR

Richard M. Dudum

Printed in the U.S.A.

For information about permission to
reproduce selections from this book:
Email: RichardDudum@MyDogThor.com

Summary: My dog Thor eats everything...almost!

Written: 1992

Published and Illustrated: 2021

ISBN: 978-0-578-95114-0

Additional art: vecteezy.com

Thank you, Randa

This book is dedicated to
all of my children and grandchildren

Read/Sing-along audio
available at Spotify.
Artist/Song:
Richard Dudum
My Dog Thor '92

I have a dog whose name is Thor.

He always eats
enough for four.

He gulps his food so fast, it's rude,

and then he begs for more.

I play a game with my dog Thor.

We use my shoes for tug of war.

But when I lose, he eats my shoes,

and then he begs for more.

Thor eats grass and daisy chains, masking tape and paper planes, rubber bands and balls of string.

# My dog eats everything.

I share a snack with my dog Thor.
I put some crackers on the floor.

But when he's through, he eats mine too,
and then he begs for more.

I teach a trick to my dog Thor.
He brings the mail to my front door.

He wags his tail, then eats my mail,
and then he begs for more.

I take a nap
with my dog Thor.

He falls asleep
and starts to snore.

But when he sleeps,
he eats my sheets,

and then he begs
for more.

I take a walk
with my dog Thor.

He finds a beehive
to explore.

He barks with glee,
then eats a bee!

And he does NOT
beg for more.

Thor eats grass and daisy chains, masking tape and paper planes, rubber bands and balls of string.

My dog eats everything.

CPSIA information can be obtained
at www.ICGtesting.com
Printed in the USA
LVHW072206060821
694775LV00006B/184